Ferries around BRITAIN

John Hendy · Miles Cowsill

Ferry Publications
PO Box 33,
Ramsey,
Isle of Man IM99 4LP
Tel: +44 (0)1624 898445
Fax: +44 (0)1624 898449
E-mail: ferrypubs@aol.com
Website: www.ferrypubs.co.uk

introduction

FERRIES AROUND BRITAIN

Since John Hendy wrote the first edition of this book in 1985 much has happened to the ships which are the subject of this publication.

A comparison with the earlier volume will reveal tremendous changes not only in the ships but also in the operators and household names such as Sealink, Townsend Thoresen and Sally Line have all passed into history. Of the vessels that remain in service, they tend to be the smaller craft and the reader will recognise Wightlink's 'Saint' and 'C' Class ships in their new liveries. The smaller ferries of the West Country have not changed much but in Scotland new and larger units have been introduced by Caledonian MacBrayne, Western Ferries and the new NorthLink service which displaced P&O Scottish Ferries in 2002.

Ferries have not only grown larger since 1985 but they have also become more comfortable. Interior design does not come under the scope of this present publication but the range of facilities, eating on board and general passenger comfort have greatly improved as ferry companies have been encouraged to compete with the airlines and the Channel Tunnel.

If they have been unable to compete in terms of speed, then they are able to offer a superior service in every other department. The Channel Tunnel has had far-reaching repercussions on all services across the English Channel. During the period after it had first opened, its effect was almost magnetic. Such was the publicity surrounding the event and the realisation that travel to the Continent was easier than it ever had been, that large numbers of people were drawn towards the Channel ports at the expense of the marginal links on either side of the Dover - Calais corridor.

Thus Newhaven - Dieppe and Ramsgate - Dunkirk/ Ostend were stretched to remain competitive and all three routes eventually succumbed in their original guises. The popular Sheerness - Vlissingen route was abandoned as a result of insoluble problems between operators Olau Line and the German unions after which their fine ships were passed to P&O at Portsmouth. Further attempts to revive the Vlissingen service with Eurolink met in failure simply because the ships were too down-market to attract the necessary traffic volumes. But growing volumes of freight have seen the emergence of TransEuropa Ferries who have made great strides with the ro-ro operation linking Ostend and Ramsgate while Transmanche Ferries from Dieppe have revived a very basic year-round service to Newhaven.

The traditional ferry ports have experienced

The ***St Clair*** at Lerwick during her last few weeks in service before the withdrawal of P&O Scottish Ferries from the Orkney and Shetland services in September 2002. She was renamed ***Barakat*** for further service in Saudi Arabia. *(Willie Mackay)*

mixed fortunes. In the days before competition when the independent UK railway companies operated ships to continue their services across the sea to Ireland or to the Continent, small and fast ships plied their trade year in year out without very much evidence that the status quo would ever change. The services were rail-connected and the importance of road communications to the ports was fairly meaningless.

Today, the siting of the historical packet ports has in some cases been more a hindrance than a help with large volumes of traffic having to find their way through urban areas to the quayside. Victorian harbours were built for Victorian ships and some, such as Folkestone and Weymouth, simply do not have the depth of water required to operate modern ferry services while dredging would simply serve to undercut the quaysides causing them to collapse.

Another traditional port to experience problems has been Liverpool. With P&O Irish Sea continuing to use the time-honoured locking-in system in and out of the River Mersey and very slow progress being made to provide the necessary deep water river ro-ro berths, the company took the totally unexpected step of switching some of their services to Mostyn in North Wales. It was fairly obvious to anyone who had ever looked at a map of the Dee estuary that dredging would be a major problem and sure enough P&O have had their share of troubles but the message to Mersey Docks is clear. Unless you can provide adequate and modern berthing facilities then we look elsewhere.

The Merchant Ferries service to Dublin has been greatly enhanced by the opening of the new Twelve Quays facility at Birkenhead and this is certainly the way ahead for operators in this busy area. Further north, the P&O service at Fleetwood continues to succeed in spite of itself but the lack of water and tortuous channel will not allow any larger tonnage to use the port and with the end of the present vessels in sight, Fleetwood's future must be fairly uncertain. The former railway port at nearby Heysham continues to be successful although its approaches are narrow and silting remains a constant problem.

At Stranraer, the lack of water has been a problem for many years and today's port facilities are antiquated. There are moves from Stena to build a new port adjacent to P&O's excellent base at Cairnryan but common sense should surely prevail and both operators should share the facilities at the latter port. The use of the HSS 1500 on the Stranraer - Belfast route is quite unsatisfactory with long periods of slow running both in Loch Ryan and Belfast Lough. With fuel costs in excess of £1 million a month, just how long the service will continue in its present form remains to be seen.

In 1985, the British ferry fleets were dominated by Sealink (the former railway shipping company) and Townsend Thoresen. The former had just been privatised and taken over by Sea Containers while the latter was proving to be the market leader with its 'Free Enterprise' brand name. How suddenly it all ended.

After an acrimonious take-over battle, Sealink came under the wing of the Swedish concern Stena Line in 1991 and after paying far too much started by closing the historic Folkestone-Boulogne service eventually abandoning the Sealink brand name in favour of their own.

As for Townsend Thoresen, their venture into the US property market proved to be their undoing and they were rescued by P&O in December 1986. Three months later came the Zeebrugge ferry disaster after which it was decided to adopt both the trading name of P&O European Ferries and a new dark blue livery.

Such was the effect of the Channel Tunnel at Dover that both P&O and Stena embarked on a joint venture in 1998 with P&O holding a 60% share. Stena's contribution shipwise was grossly inferior to the input of the market leader and the Stena units that remained were refurbished to bring them up to an acceptable standard.

Top: The ***St. Catherine*** and the ***St. Faith*** are seen here at Portsmouth Gunwharf. Today, Wightlink maintain their Portsmouth-Fishbourne service with five vessels. *(John Hendy)*

With the joint venture being abandoned in 2002, P&O Ferries have rebranded themselves as a result of which both the Hull and Portsmouth operations now come under the management of

NORMANDIE
NORMANDIE
TUG

The ***Normandie*** makes a splendid sight as she leaves Portsmouth on a morning sailing for Caen in July 2002. *(John Hendy)*

Dover. Stena Line continues to operate the Hook of Holland - Harwich/ Immingham services and has a presence on the Irish Sea at Fishguard, Holyhead and Stranraer but a year is a long time in the ferry world and change can happen quickly.

Another revolution in the British ferry scene will immediately become obvious if further comparisons with 1985 are made. The fast ferry had been in use in the Channel Islands and to the Isle of Wight without any large scale impact on the rest of the country. The SRN 4 hovercraft at Dover had, since 1969, provided a niche market but there were no moves to extend this until Tasmanian fast craft manufacturers International Catamarans (InCat) supplied the 74 metre Hoverspeed Great Britain to Sea Containers in 1990. In spite of their high fuel costs, constant maintenance, poor performance in bad weather and limited life span, certain ferry operators went overboard to commit themselves to the sudden onrush of assorted designs that flooded the market. It must be said that in the builders' haste to produce designs and the owners' to acquire them, there were many craft that put to sea without sufficient periods of evaluation. This resulted in cancelled and unreliable services and technical problems galore. Of course there is a place for the fast craft but only where it has the luxury of a conventional ferry to support it and provide back-up so that if there are problems then customers will not be inconvenienced. This has been a hard lesson for some while others eg Commodore Ferries, wisely purchased a ro-pax ferry to support their catamarans. Other operators have been slow to learn from their mistakes.

The introduction of the new Superfast ferries on the overnight Rosyth - Zeebrugge link and the ordering of the Pont Aven by Brittany Ferries surely point to the future: conventional ferries complete with all the facilities passengers have been educated to expect but with engines able to drive the ships at speeds around 30 knots. Other long-haul operators will doubtless watch the progress of the Pont Aven with interest and if she succeeds then we may expect to see further vessels of this type.

The ***European Seaway*** and the ***P&OSL Dover*** arrive at Calais inward bound from Dover. *(John Hendy)*

The Lower Dart ferry makes a picturesque scene as she arrives at Kingswear. *(John Hendy)*

The future appears bright. Although modern day ferries may lack the flair and lines of their predecessors, they are without doubt the most comfortable and versatile of ships yet supplied to their owners. In our clockwise journey around Britain, we have included a complete range of ferry types - from the cross-Channel super ferry to the small estuarine chain ferry, from the compact and spartan island ferry to the HSS and the purely roll on-roll off freighter.

We hope that our readers will enjoy our selection as they travel in the **Ferries around Britain.**

Miles Cowsill,
Ramsey,
Isle of Man.

John Hendy,
Ivychurch,
Kent.

An artist's impression of the new ***Pride of Canterbury/Pride of Kent*** due to enter service in April/May 2003. *(P&O Ferries)*

Caledonian MacBrayne

The ***Hebridean Isles*** arrives at Port Askaig (Islay) from Kennacraig with the Paps of Jura in the background. *(Miles Cowsill)*

THAMES ESTUARY

Left: The ***Ernest Bevin***, ***James Newman*** (pictured here) and the ***John Burns*** were built for London County Council in 1963. Today the vessels are operated by the London Borough of Greenwich, who operate the service on behalf of the Department of Transport. The five minute Woolwich Free Ferry across the Thames is a useful alternative to the nearby Blackwall Tunnel. Each vessel can carry 32 cars and 6 lorries and at the grand age of 39 years still offers valiant service on the Thames. *(Ferry Publications Library)*

Below: The ***Duchess M*** is the latest in a long line of passenger vessels to operate the Tilbury-Gravesend ferry. She was built as the ***Vesta*** in 1956 by Camper & Nicholson for the Port of Portsmouth Steam Launch & Towing Co. Ltd's Gosport ferry service. Sold in 1974 for pleasure use on the Thames, she later moved northwards to the River Tyne before taking up a cruising role in the River Medway area of Kent in 1996. (*John Bryant)*

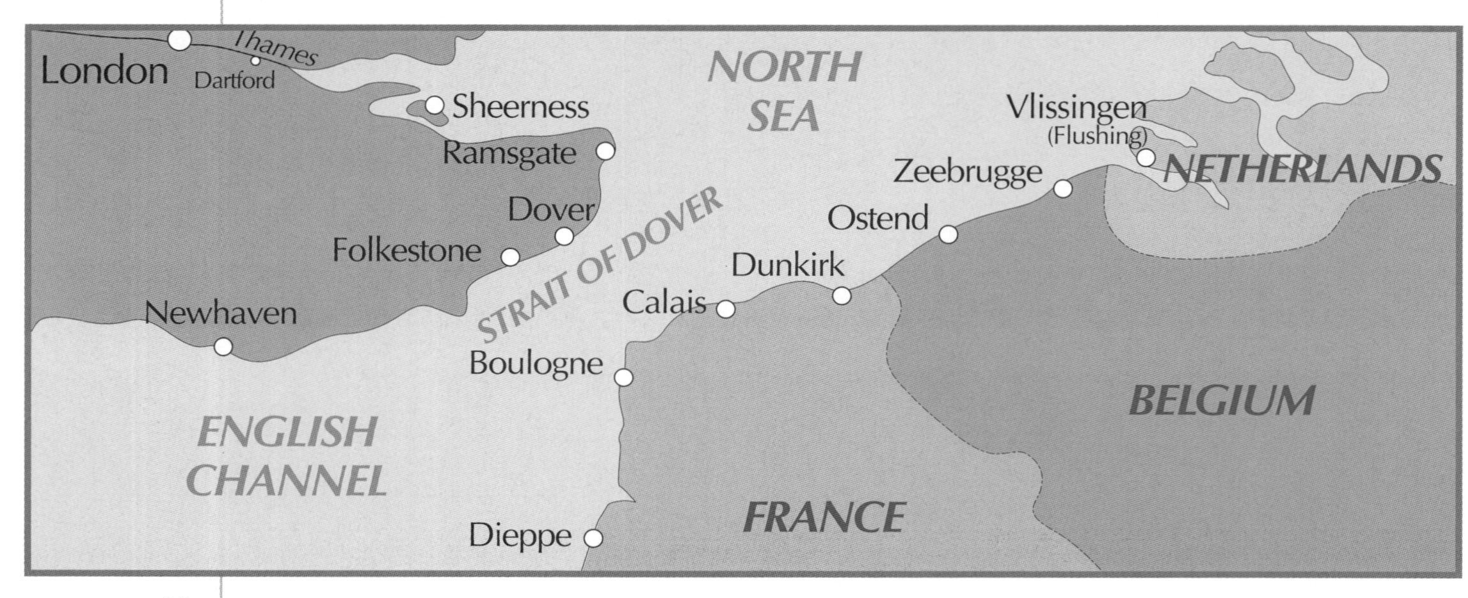

Top Right: During the last seven years, Dartford has blossomed as an important port for ro-ro operations to Belgium and Holland. Today Dart Line operate seven freight vessels which serve the ports of Zeebrugge and Vlissingen. One of the three ships acquired from China is illustrated here in this view, the ***Dart 8***, originally built as the ***XI Feng Ku***. All three vessels were built as deep-sea ro-ro container vessels for service from China to Australia and New Zealand. In 1999 the vessels were purchased by Dart Line. They can accommodate 12 passengers and can carry up to 155 trailers. *(John Hendy)*

Right: A series of eight vessels was built in Romania as the 'Bazias' sisters for operations in the Mediterranean. Today Dart Line have four of the vessels on their links. One of the earlier sisters, ***Bazias 1,*** is pictured here at the Dartford Terminal prior to her departure to Zeebrugge. *(John Bryant)*

Below: Another port on the lower Thames which has expanded in recent years is Purfleet and its growth has been due to Cobelfret Ferries. The Belgian company operates from Purfleet to Zeebrugge daily and had the contract to transport Ford motor cars from the Dagenham factory to Europe until February 2002. The company have recently introduced a series of new ships and one of the more modern units, the ***Victorine***, is pictured loading for Zeebrugge. The Japanese-built ship can accommodate up to 630 cars or 157 trailers. *(John Bryant)*

THAMES & SHEERNESS

Left: Possibly one of the most attractive classes of vessel to operate in the last thirty years out of the Thames estuary was operated by Swedish Lloyd. Three similar ships were built for the company and offered a standard and a class of accommodation far ahead of their time when they entered service in 1967. The ***Patricia*** opened the first ferry link between Southampton and Bilbao in 1966, while her sisters the ***Saga*** (pictured here) and ***Svea*** operated from the Thames from Tilbury to Gothenburg, a service which was only to last until 1971. The ***Svea*** was owned by Svea Line but was later purchased and became the ***Hispania.***. *(FotoFlite)*

Below: Union problems and high running costs of Olau Line's operations between Sheerness and Vlissingen were to close the route in May 1994. The ***Olau Hollandia*** and ***Olau Britannia*** offered an excellent standard of service. Both vessels were later chartered to P&O Portsmouth for their Le Havre operation. The ***Olau Hollandia*** is seen prior to entering service and berthed at the new Sheerness linkspan while her older namesake is leaving the port for the last time before her new career in the Baltic as the ***Nordlandia***. *(FotoFlite)*

RAMSGATE

Top Right: The port of Ramsgate has had mixed fortunes since it was established as a ferry port in 1980. Following the demise of RMT's operations in 1998 and that of Sally in 1999, the Slovenian company, TransEuropa Shipping Line, established their own service from Ramsgate to Ostend in Belgium. Where others have failed, this company appears to have established the port and expanded its operations. Ironically, the company operate two former RMT vessels, the ***Eurovoyager*** and ***Primrose***. The ***Eurovoyager,*** formerly the ***Prins Albert***, was built for the state-owned Belgian company for their Ostend-Dover service in 1978. In 1998 she was sold to the Slovenian company. *(John Hendy)*

Right: Following the demise of Holyman Ferries, Sea Containers acquired the interests of the fast ferry service to the Belgian port of Ostend. Both InCat craft from Holyman were initially placed on the Dover-Ostend service but due to lack of traffic the ***Rapide*** was transferred to the Irish Sea. The ***Diamant*** today maintains the seasonal service to Ostend. She is seen leaving Ostend in her first livery of Sea Containers. The service closed at the end of the 2002 season. *(John Hendy)*

Below: The ***Laburnum*** was transferred from the Adriatic in 2001 to operate on the TransEuropa Shipping Lines service from Ostend to Ramsgate. This vessel is no stranger to the English Channel as she was originally built for Townsend as ***Free Enterprise V***. Following the demise of Townsend Thoresen and the rebranding of the company under P&O European Ferries, the vessel was renamed ***Pride of Hythe***. She left Ostend for a Genoa-Tangiers charter early in 2003. *(John Hendy)*

OLEANDER

The ***Oleander*** (ex ***Pride of Free Enterprise***, ex ***Pride of Bruges***, ex ***P&OSL Picardy***) was sold by P&O Stena Line in 2001 for further service on the English Channel between Ramsgate and Ostend. The vessel is seen shortly after entering service with TransEuropa Ferries. *(FotoFlite)*

Top Left: The port of Ostend has also enjoyed mixed fortunes since the closure of RMT's operations in 1997. With the expansion of TransEuropa Shipping Lines' operations in the last couple of years, the port authorities have been anxious to see another operator at Ostend. In 2000 they were successful in securing Ferryways who chartered two well known English Channel ro-ro vessels, the ***Gabriele Wehr*** and ***Thomas Wehr***, both of which were built for the Wehr Transport Company during the late 70s. The ***Anglian Way*** (ex ***Thomas Wehr***) pictured here, has had a career with many of the leading shipping companies in the UK. In 1982 she was chartered to Tor Line; in 1986 she saw service with North Sea Ferries during the lengthening of the ***Norland*** and ***Norstar***. Further charters followed over the next couple of years in Europe and in 1995 she was again operating under the banner of P&O on their Felixstowe-Zeebrugge route, until the end of 1999. *(FotoFlite)*

Left: The opening of the Channel Tunnel brought the end for Sally Line's Ramsgate-Dunkirk service. The port really never made the impression of its contemporaries further down the Channel and poor road communications were to ultimately to lead to its demise. In a last ditch attempt Sally Line marketed themselves as Sally Direct, based on a similar concept to the cheap airline business, and opened a service to Ostend. The ***Eurotraveller*** is seen here in the company's Sally Direct livery outward bound from Ramsgate.She sails today as TransEuropa's ***Larkspur*** *(FotoFlite)*

Bottom: The ***Stena Nordica*** opened the 5 hour Tilbury-Calais service in 1965. The route was marketed as 'The Londoner' and the French-built ship accommodated 935 passengers and 129 cars. Chartered to the Stranraer - Larne route in 1966, Stena brought in even smaller tonnage before the link was closed at the end of the 1967 season. Her sister ***Stena Danica*** operated a freight service between Dover and Zeebrugge for Townsend Car Ferries. *(FotoFlite)*

DOVER

Above: In the early 90s, P&O European Ferries ordered a series of four ro-pax vessels from Germany for their Dover-Zeebrugge service to replace the smaller European Class vessels on the route. Following the introduction of three of the vessels and the need for additional tonnage on the Dover-Calais service, the fourth in this Class was modified to be a passenger ferry. Originally the 'Burgundy' was to be named ***European Causeway*** for the Zeebrugge service. The ***Pride of Burgundy*** as she was originally named for the Dover-Calais route entered service on the Dover Strait in 1993. Following the merger of P&O European Ferries and Stena Line the vessel was renamed ***P&OSL Burgundy***. *(John Hendy)*

Below: The ***European Highway***, (pictured), ***European Pathway*** and ***European Seaway*** were the mainstay of the Dover-Zeebrugge freight service until 15th December 2002. In Summer 2002 it was announced that two of these freight ships would be converted to passenger mode for the Calais route, to replace the 'Kent' and the 'Canterbury', following the decision to close the Zeebrugge service after 36 years. *(FotoFlite)*

Below: Norfolkline commenced operations from Dover in 2000 and have quietly expanded their operations under the noses of P&O Stena Line, SeaFrance and Hoverspeed. Originally dismissed as a short-term player, Norfolkline have expanded and improved their operations radically during their two years at Dover. Their success is partly due to a market demand for a cheaper style operation and also the need for more freight capacity on the Dover Strait. Overwhelmingly their success has been due to the charter of the two Merchant Ferries ships built in Spain. Both the ***Midnight Merchant*** and ***Northern Merchant*** have proved ideal for the Dunkirk route, with their excellent service speed of 22.5 knots. In October 2002 a third vessel in the class, ***Dawn Merchant***, joined the operations from the Irish Sea. *(FotoFlite)*

Below: Possibly two of the most successful vessels built for the Dover Strait in the last 15 years have been the ***Pride of Dover*** (pictured here) and ***Pride of Calais***. The order for the construction of these two ships was made by Townsend Thoresen and the first of these vessels, the ***Pride of Dover*** appeared in their orange hull livery. With the takeover of the company by P&O in 1987, the second ship, the ***Pride of Calais***, entered operations in the P&O dark blue livery. Both purpose-built ships have been extremely successful on the Dover-Calais service and have performed far in excess of expectations. *(Miles Cowsill)*

Below: The ***Nord Pas-de-Calais*** was ordered by SNCF to operate on the train ferry service between Dunkirk and Dover. With the opening of the Channel Tunnel, the vessel was not immediately withdrawn from the train ferry service as a role was found for her to continue operations on the link to convey road vehicles and dangerous loads, which at the time were banned from the Tunnel. During December 1995, the train ferry service finished between the UK and France and a further new role was found for the eight year old ship. In February 1996 she was renamed ***SeaFrance Nord-Pas-de-Calais*** and switched permanently to the Calais-Dover freight service. The company have plans to extend her accommodation in the near future so she can be used as a ro-pax vessel. *(John Hendy)*

Below: The ***SeaFrance Manet*** was built by SNCF as the ***Champs Elysees*** for their Calais-Dover and Boulogne-Dover services. In an effort to boost the flagging Dieppe-Newhaven route, the vessel was transferred in 1990 to the Normandy operation. With mounting losses two years later, SNCF withdrew from the Newhaven-Dieppe route and Stena Sealink Line took over the operation and renamed her the ***Stena Parisien***. In 1997 the charter was terminated by Stena Line and she returned to the Dover Strait, renamed ***SeaFrance Manet***. *(John Hendy)*

Above: Possibly the most attractive of all the vessels currently running on the Dover-Calais route is the ***SeaFrance Renoir***. The vessel was originally built as the ***Cote d'Azur*** in 1981 to operate the 'Flagship Service' in tandem with the new Sealink vessels ***St. Anselm*** and ***St. Christopher***. The ***SeaFrance Renoir*** has never operated on any other route apart from the Calais service. With the introduction of the ***SeaFrance Rodin***, she is to become the relief and standby vessel for the company. *(Miles Cowsill)*

Left: Much to the disappointment of many travellers on the Dover Strait, Hoverspeed withdrew their hovercraft service in 2000 in favour of using their SuperSeaCat vessels. The success of the hovercraft on the Dover-Calais service could not be matched by the SuperSeaCats due partly to their inflexibility in loading. In 2002 the company decided to reintroduce their older InCat craft on the Dover-Calais route. The oldest of these craft, ***Hoverspeed Great Britain***, launched as the ***Christopher Columbus*** and winner of the Hales Trophy - the Atlantic 'Blue Riband' remains on the Dover Strait. Of all the InCat vessels, the 'HGB' has had the most interesting of careers and has the added accolade of gaining back the Hales Trophy from the SS ***United States***. She then inaugurated a fast ferry service from Portsmouth to Cherbourg which proved an operational disaster. Later she was transferred to the Dover Strait to operate in tandem with the hovercraft services to Boulogne and Calais. The vessel was to see a series of charters in 1992/3 in Argentina and in the summer was used to provide additional sailings between Belfast and Stranraer, transferring back to the Channel later the same year. She has since that date remained on the Dover Strait operating principally from Folkestone until the port's demise in Autumn 2000. During Summer 2001 she operated the newly-established route of Sea Containers between Heysham and Belfast. For 2002 she operated alongside the ***SeaCat Danmark*** and ***Atlantic II***. *(John Hendy)*

Above: The ***P&OSL Aquitaine*** was originally built as the ***Prins Filip*** for RMT for their Ostend-Dover service. Although completed in 1991, she did not enter service until May 1992. The new flagship of the Ostend-Dover Line never really made the impression she should have, as ideally a second sister should have been built to operate alongside her, but there were no state funds at the time to build an identical ship for the route. After only six years in service she was withdrawn from operations and offered for sale following the demise of RMT. In 1998 she was acquired by the Stena Group and renamed ***Stena Royal.*** In the November she was chartered to P&O Stena Line to operate as a freight-only vessel on their Dover-Zeebrugge service. During the next spring P&O Stena Line decided to charter the vessel on a long-term basis and she was renamed ***P&OSL Aquitaine***. Today she forms an integral part of P&O Stena Line's operations between Dover and Calais but is due to be withdrawn in 2005. *(Miles Cowsill)*

Right: The ***P&OSL Provence*** was originally built as the ***Stena Jutlandica***, with the ***Stena Danica*** her identical sister, for Stena Line service between Gothenburg and Frederikshavn. With the introduction of the HSS service between Denmark and Sweden and Stena Line's desire to expand their Dover-Calais service, the ***Stena Jutlandica*** was transferred from the Baltic to the English Channel in 1996 and renamed ***Stena Empereur***. Two years later Stena Line's operations on the Dover Strait were merged with P&O to form P&O Stena Line. In 1998 she was renamed ***P&OSL Provence*** and ***Pride of Provence*** in 2003. *(John Hendy)*

SEALINK
BRITISH
FERRIES

The ***St. Anselm*** and ***St. Christopher*** were built for Sealink to compete with the new Townsend Thoresen Spirit Class introduced from 1979. The ***St. Christopher*** is pictured arriving at Calais in 1989 from Dover. *(Miles Cowsill)*

Above: The ***Chartres*** was built as a multi-purpose vessel for Dover-Calais, the Folkestone-Boulogne service and also as relief vessel on the Dover-Dunkirk train ferry service. With the opening of the Channel Tunnel, she was employed initially to handle train-connected passengers before the Tunnel was fully operational. The vessel makes a fine sight here as she leaves Calais during her last season. *(Miles Cowsill)*

Above: The Dover-Dunkirk train ferry service closed in 1995 following the opening of the Channel Tunnel. During the route's history there have been many interesting vessels on the link and possibly one of the most famous was the French registered ***Saint-Germain***. The Danish-built vessel arrives here from Dover in 1986, her penultimate season on the link. *(Miles Cowsill)*

Right: The ***Stena Fantasia*** will not go down in the history books as one of the most attractive vessels on the Dover Strait, however the converted ro-ro vessel has proved very successful on the Dover-Calais service. With the merger of Stena Line and P&O's operations, she was renamed ***P&OSL Canterbury***. During 2003 she is due to be withdrawn from service. *(Miles Cowsill)*

Below: The 'Spirit Class' vessels were built for Townsend Thoresen to replace the 'Free Enterprise' Class vessels on the Dover-Calais route. The first of this Class, the ***Spirit of Free Enterprise***, is seen outward bound from Calais to Dover. *(Miles Cowsill)*

FOLKESTONE

Above: The ***Stena Hengist*** leaves Folkestone for Boulogne in her last season. Stena Line took the decision to close the Folkestone-Boulogne service at the end of 1991 as a cost-saving measure and since that date the port has never really recovered despite a number of different operators trying to make a success of it. Today the harbour facilities are no longer used and with the success and expansion of Dover it is unlikely that the port will ever establish itself again as a cross-Channel terminal. *(Miles Cowsill)*

Left: This interesting aerial view shows the ro-ro vessel ***Purbeck*** (on charter to Falcon Freight) and the ***Hoverspeed Great Britain*** at Folkestone Harbour. *(FotoFlite)*

NEWHAVEN

Right: Possibly the most picturesque route in the English Channel is the Newhaven-Dieppe service. The link was plagued during the 60s and the 70s with industrial action, which eventually was to see the withdrawal of the joint ferry service of SNCF and Sealink. The route fared little better under the management of Stena Line and later P&O Stena Line due to pressure from the operations at Dover and Portsmouth following the opening of the Channel Tunnel. Following the withdrawal of P&O Stena Line, Sea Containers commenced a fast ferry operation for the summer period only. With demands on both sides of the Channel to re-establish the service as an all-year round operation and freight link, Transmanche Ferries stepped in. The route today is maintained by the ro-pax ***Dieppe*** and the ***Sardinia Vera***, (pictured) which was originally built for Stena Line as the ***Stena Atlantica***. With the Channel Tunnel nearly at capacity, and both Dover and Portsmouth regaining similar levels of traffic to those prior to the opening of the Channel Tunnel, the Newhaven-Dieppe link has become more attractive for freight hauliers. *(John Hendy)*

Above: In Summer 2001 the ***Diamant*** was transferred to the Newhaven-Dieppe route following the withdrawal of P&O Stena Line from the link in the previous year. In 2002 the route was operated by the ***SuperSeaCat One*** which is seen arriving at Dieppe. *(John Hendy)*

Stena Sealink
STENA PARISIEN

The ***Stena Parisien*** moving berths at Dieppe following the opening of the port's new linkspan and to celebrate the new service operated by Stena Sealink Line. *(John Hendy)*

Above: This view shows the ***Stena Londoner*** arriving at Dieppe following Stena Line's opening of the service. The route was to close with the ***Stena Cambria*** in 1999 following the merger of Stena Line with P&O. *(Miles Cowsill)*

Below: Happier times at Dieppe. The French registered ***Senlac*** leaves her home port for Newhaven on her four hour crossing to Sussex. *(Miles Cowsill)*

PORTSMOUTH

Above: The ***Mont St. Michel*** eventually entered service on 20th December 2002 after a nine month delay at her builders Van der Giessen-de Noord. The vessel was built to replace the ***Duc de Normandie*** (ex ***Prinses Beatrix***) on the Caen service and now operates in tandem with the ***Normandie***. The ***Mont St. Michel*** can accommodate 2,120 passengers and 600 cars. *(Brittany Ferries)*

Right: Prior to the introduction of the ***Mont St Michel***, Brittany Ferries chartered the much-travelled ***Purbeck*** to offer additional capacity on their Caen-Portsmouth service for freight. The ***Purbeck*** was originally built for Truckline Ferries for their Cherbourg-Poole service. During 1986 she was lengthened to increase her freight capacity. Some six years later, she was to see service between Roscoff, Plymouth and Santander. In 1994, she was sold to Channel Island Ferries to operate the freight service between Poole and the Channel Islands. A year later following the demise of BCIF, she was chartered to Sally Ferries for use on their Dartford-Vlissingen service. Since then she has seen a variety of charters in UK waters including Irish Ferries, Gaelic Ferries and Falcon Seafreight. Her future is currently unknown but such a versatile ship will surely find further work. *(John Bryant)*

Below: The ***Bretagne*** was built by Brittany Ferries as a replacement vessel for the ***Quiberon*** on the Plymouth-Santander and Roscoff-Cork services. With increased demand on both the Spanish and Irish services, Brittany Ferries introduced the ***Val de Loire*** to replace her in 1993. The ***Bretagne*** was then transferred to the St. Malo-Portsmouth service, replacing two older vessels in the fleet.She has proved an overwhelming success on the St. Malo service and it is likely in the future that a second vessel will be introduced on the route to support her. *(Miles Cowsill)*

Below: The ***Duc de Normandie*** (ex ***Prinses Beatrix***) was built for the Hook of Holland - Harwich service for SMZ. When she was purchased by Brittany Ferries in 1985 she was to open their highly successful Caen route a year later. Today she is on the Roscoff - Plymouth service and it seems likely that she will be replaced by the ***Bretagne*** in 2004 and withdrawn from the fleet. *(John Hendy)*

Above: The ***Normandie*** leaves Portsmouth for Caen. The vessel has been employed on the link since 1992. *(Miles Cowsill)*

Left: An artist's impression of Brittany Ferries' new ***Pont-Aven*** which is due to enter service with the company in 2004. *(Brittany Ferries)*

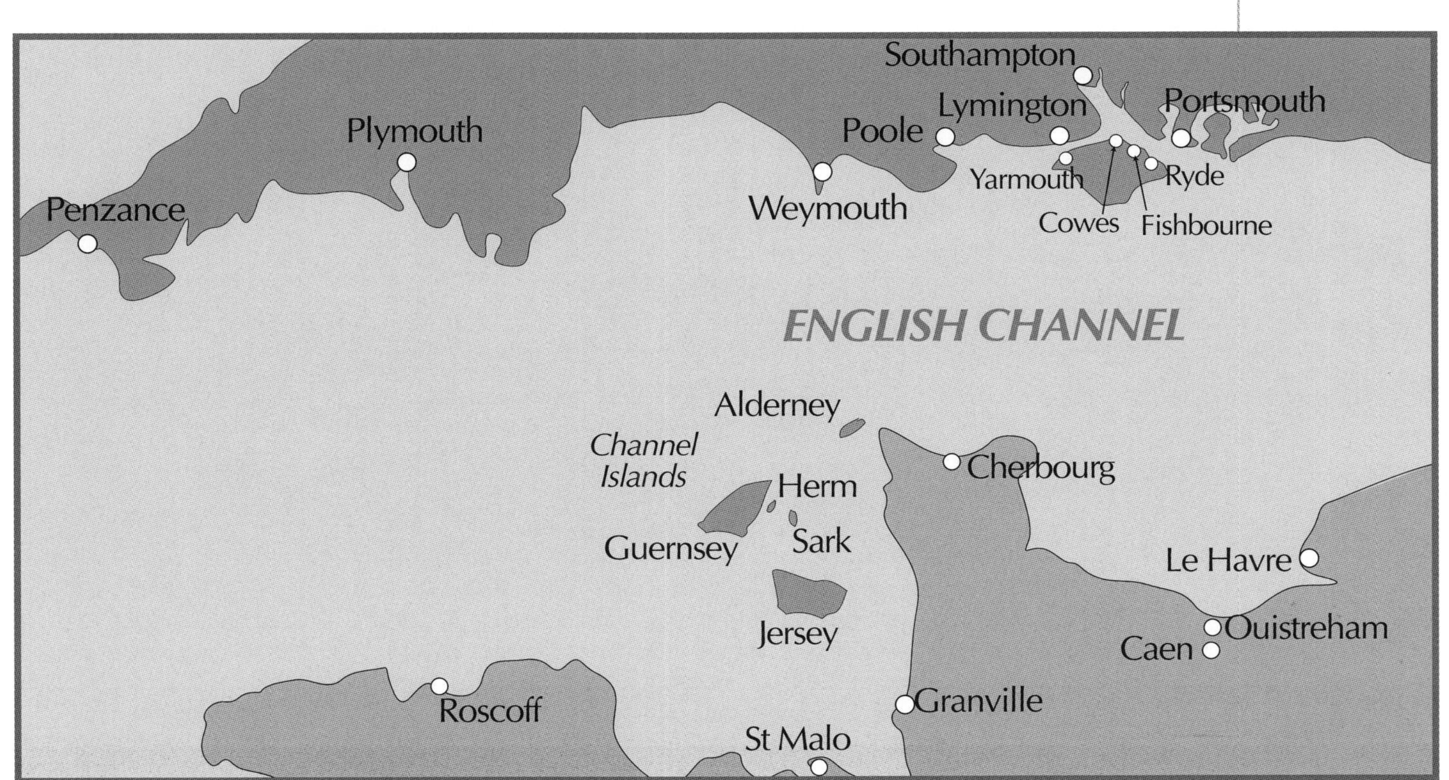

Above: In 1993 P&O European Ferries opened a new ferry link between Portsmouth and Bilbao in northern Spain to rival their competitors, Brittany Ferries, who had established their own Spanish service in 1978. The then giant ferry ***Olympia*** was initially chartered from Viking Line to open this new 36 hour link between the UK and Spain. She was renamed ***Pride of Bilbao*** and is able to carry 2,553 passengers and 600 cars; today she maintains two weekly round sailings to Spain and one round trip at the weekends to Cherbourg. During her charter to P&O, the vessel has changed ownership and today forms part of the Irish Ferries' fleet. *(Miles Cowsill)*

Above: Following Sea Containers' disastrous season between Portsmouth and Cherbourg in 1990 using the ***Hoverspeed Great Britain***, P&O Portsmouth introduced their own fast ferry service between both ports using the ***Superstar Express*** in 1998. Following the success of the fast ferry operation, a larger craft was sought for the route. The ***Portsmouth Express*** was built as the ***Catalonia*** for service between Barcelona and Mallorca. In April 2000 she was chartered to P&O Portsmouth. The 91 metre InCat craft is able to achieve a service speed of 41 knots and can carry 920 passengers and 225 cars. During the winter periods of 2000/2001, she has seen service in South America when the Portsmouth-Cherbourg fast ferry service was closed. *(Chris Randall)*

Right:: Following the introduction of the ***Ulysses,*** the ***Isle of Innisfree*** was withdrawn from service and offered for sale. In late February 2002 P&O Portsmouth chartered the vessel to replace the old 'Super Viking' vessels on the Cherbourg route. After modifications and improvements, the vessel entered service in September 2002 as the ***Pride of Cherbourg***. *(Miles Cowsill)*

Below: The 'Super Viking' vessels were built for Townsend Thoresen in the mid-70s. Two of the vessels were subsequently jumboised in 1986 for the Le Havre route. Following the introduction of the former Olau ships, both jumboised 'Super Vikings' ***Pride of Cherbourg*** (ex ***Viking Valiant***) and ***Pride of Hampshire*** (ex ***Viking Venturer***, ex ***Pride of Le Havre***) were then transferred to the Cherbourg service in 1994. Both vessels have given valiant service on the link for the company and were withdrawn in September 2002. This view shows the renamed ***Pride of Cherbourg A*** arriving immediately prior to her withdrawal. *(Miles Cowsill)*

Top Right: Built as one of four similar ships for TT Line of Germany to operate for their Olau Line between Sheerness and Vlissingen, in May 1994 when the Dutch link was closed, the 'Hollandia' and her sister the 'Britannia' were chartered to P&O European Ferries. The ***Olau Hollandia*** was renamed ***Pride of Le Havre*** and her sister was renamed ***Pride of Portsmouth*** (pictured here). Today both vessels maintain the Le Havre operation together. *(John Hendy)*

Below: The ***Commodore Clipper*** leaves St Peter Port en route to Jersey. The vessel is a near sister to the ***Ben-my-Chree*** - see page 75. *(John Hendy)*

Below: Following the demise of British Channel Island Ferries, a joint ferry operation between Commodore Ferries and Condor was established to serve the Channel Islands from the UK. Initially, two multi-purpose freight ships were built to handle all freight operations from Portsmouth to the Islands. The two vessels built in Holland, the ***Commodore Goodwill*** and ***Commodore Clipper***, proved extremely successful and reliable on the routes. With the demand for a conventional ship to maintain the services to Jersey and Guernsey, Commodore Ferries built a ro-pax vessel at Van der Giessen de Noord to operate alongside their freight operations. The first sister, the ***Commodore Clipper***, was sold by the company on the entry into service of the new ro-pax vessel and today the 'Goodwill' maintains the overnight services from the UK to Guernsey and Jersey. The current ***Commodore Clipper*** is also employed to maintain the Jersey-St. Malo link at the weekends. *(Chris Randall)*

Above: The ***Viking Victory*** *(*ex ***Viking I****)* opened the Portsmouth-Cherbourg service in 1976. The Norwegian vessel is seen here leaving Portsmouth during her first season. The ship entered service from Southampton in 1964. *(Miles Cowsill)*

Below: Following the merger with P&O Normandy Ferries, both the ***Dragon*** and the ***Leopard*** were transferred to the Townsend Thoresen fleet to operate from Portsmouth. The attractive-looking ***Dragon*** is seen inward bound from Le Havre as the BCIF ***Corbiere*** is outward bound on her morning sailing to Jersey and Guernsey. *(Miles Cowsill)*

TT
TOWNSEND THORESEN

The ***Viking Venturer*** (pictured here) and the ***Viking Valiant*** were built for the Southampton-Cherbourg service and were transferred to Portsmouth in 1984. The 'Venturer' is seen here outward bound for Le Havre prior to her jumboisation. (*Miles Cowsill)*

Above: Possibly one of the most successful vessels in the early stages of Brittany Ferries was the ***Armorique***. The Norwegian-built vessel was to operate on all the company's routes and was to open both the St. Malo and Santander links.This view shows her leaving Portsmouth in the company's original livery. Today, the vessel is employed on a ferry service between Hong Kong and mainland China. *(Miles Cowsill)*

Left: This interesting picture shows the ***Earl Granville*** swinging off the berth at Portsmouth for Cherbourg in British Ferries' livery. Following the huge losses within the Sealink Group in 1984, the Western Channel operations were branded 'British Ferries'. Sadly, Sealink's involvement in the Channel Islands was to terminate at the end of the 1986 season. *(Miles Cowsill)*

Below: During the peak periods on the Portsmouth-Le Havre service, both Townsend Thoresen and P&O have had to charter additional tonnage to handle freight traffic on the link. The ***Viking Trader*** is seen here inward bound from Le Havre whilst on charter on the link. This picture shows her in Townsend Thoresen livery but with a P&O flag on her funnel following the takeover of Townsend Thoresen by P&O in 1986. The ***Viking Trader***, later named ***European Navigator,*** has recently been withdrawn from service from P&O Irish Sea's operations. The vessel was sold to Jordanian interests in 2003 and operates now as the ***Black Iris.*** *(Miles Cowsill)*

PORTSMOUTH/ISLE OF WIGHT

Top Right: The services to the Isle of Wight have become more intense over the last 25 years with the growing demand from holidaymakers and freight operators. Prior to the demise of the nationalised company Sealink and the sale to Sea Containers, two purpose-built ships, the ***St. Helen*** and ***St. Catherine***, were built for the Portsmouth-Fishbourne service. The distinctive-looking vessels which are able to carry 142 cars were joined later by two further sisters of a similar design and concept. The ***St. Helen*** is pictured here leaving Portsmouth in the company's latest livery, which includes their website address for online bookings. *(John Hendy)*

Right: The ***St. Cecilia*** swings off her berth at Portsmouth's Gunwharf. *(John Hendy)*

Below: In 2001 even larger tonnage was introduced on the Portsmouth-Fishbourne service. The 3,500 gross ton ***St. Clare*** is seen arriving at Portsmouth from the Isle of Wight. The Polish-built ship is able to accommodate 750 passengers and 180 cars. *(Miles Cowsill)*

Top Left: Following the withdrawal of the conventional classic passenger services operated by the ***Southsea*** and ***Brading***, two fast craft built in Australia were introduced on the passenger operation between Portsmouth and Ryde Pier. The InCat craft, ***Our Lady Pamela*** and ***Our Lady Patricia***, are able to achieve the crossing between the mainland and the Island in 15 minutes and can accommodate up to 410 passengers. *(John Hendy)*

Left: In Summer 2000 the company acquired two Singaporian fast craft, the ***Water Jet 1*** and ***Water Jet 2,*** which had operated in the Philippines after their construction. Wightlink acquired both vessels to replace the older InCat craft on the Ryde service; both ships have not proved ideal for the route, so much so that the company have been forced to maintain the older InCat craft in reserve to back up the newly acquired vessels.*(John Hendy)*

Below: Hovertravel operate a rival service to that of Wightlink between Southsea and Ryde using a variety of hovercraft, including the ***Double O Seven*** and the ***Freedom 90*** (pictured here). The company plan to introduce two new hovercraft on the route in the near future. *(John Hendy)*

Top Right: Another busy commuter link in the Solent area is the operation between Portsmouth and Gosport. This service has been operated for many years by the ***Gosport Queen*** and ***Portsmouth Queen*** (pictured here), both built in 1966. During 2001 the company introduced a replacement vessel the ***Spirit of Portsmouth***, which is able to carry an additional 50 passengers to the older sisters. It had originally been planned that a second new vessel would be placed on the route but it seems likely that either the ***Gosport Queen*** or ***Portsmouth Queen*** will continue to operate alongside the new ship. *(John Hendy)*

Right: The Gosport ferry company is not just restricted to offering services across the Harbour between Portsmouth and Gosport. The excursion vessel ***Solent Enterprise*** is employed to work around the Solent and Portsmouth Harbour. *(Andrew Cooke)*

Below: Not classed as a ferry, but an important part of the UK passenger scene, is the attractive looking paddle steamer, ***Waverley***. The 1947-built vessel is seen leaving Portsmouth during one of her autumn excursions on the south coast. *(Miles Cowsill)*

SOUTHAMPTON/ISLE OF WIGHT

Below: Red Funnel Ferries are the main ferry company to rival Wightlink on the Isle of Wight services. Much starved of capital finance in the 80's, it was not until 1994 that newer tonnage was introduced. The first of these vessels, the ***Red Falcon***, brought a significant increase in capacity for the company followed by her sister, the ***Red Osprey*** (pictured), both of which are able to carry 140 cars and 895 passengers.Two years later a third sister the ***Red Eagle*** was introduced on the Southampton-East Cowes service. Plans to stretch the sisters and raise their car capacity to 200 were announced during late 2002. The three ferries are able to maintain an hourly operation on the 55 minute crossing to the Isle of Wight. *(Miles Cowsill)*

Above: White Horse Ferries maintain the year-round passenger operation between Southampton and Hythe using the 10 year old catamaran vessel ***Great Expectations*** and the traditionally-built passenger ship the ***Hotspur IV*** from 1946. *(Miles Cowsill)*

In tandem with the car ferry service, Red Funnel operate a fast ferry service using three catamaran vessels ***Red Jet 1***, ***Red Jet 2*** and ***Red Jet 3*** which were built locally at Cowes on the Isle of Wight. These craft are able to maintain a schedule of 20 minutes to Cowes and are a valuable asset to Islanders who work in Southampton. A further craft has since been built in Australia. *(John Hendy)*

The ***Red Falcon*** outward bound from Cowes to Southampton. *(John Hendy)*

RED FUNNEL
3

A classic view of the ***Netley Castle*** inward bound to Cowes from Southampton in 1994. The vessel today is employed in Croatia. *(John Hendy)*

ISLE OF WIGHT

Above: The chain ferry service between East and West Cowes is an important link for the commercial users and residents alike. The current vessel ***No 5*** was built in East Cowes for the Isle of Wight Council in 1976 and is able to carry 15 cars. *(Miles Cowsill)*

Above Right: The third ferry service across to the Isle of Wight is operated by Wightlink from the attractive ports of Lymington and Yarmouth. The company have been unable to replace the tonnage on this picturesque route due to environmentalist pressures and still maintain the 70s built ***Caedmon***, ***Cenred*** and ***Cenwulf*** (pictured here). The route is in danger of closing if newer and more effective tonnage is not introduced in the near future on this 30 minute crossing. *(John Hendy)*

Above: The first diesel ferry built for the Portsmouth-Ryde route was the ***Southsea*** (1948-1988), seen here laid up at Newhaven awaiting her fate. The vessel has recently been towed to Portsmouth following her acquisition by a group of enthusiasts intent on restoring her. *(John Hendy)*

POOLE

Right: The Dorset port of Poole established itself as a ferry port for passengers in 1989 when BCIF decided to transfer their operations from Portsmouth to reduce their crossing times to the Channel Islands. With the demise of BCIF in 1994, Condor Ferries introduced their fast ferry operations from the port to Jersey and Guernsey. Today the two InCat craft ***Condor Express*** and ***Condor Vitesse*** (pictured here) maintain the link for the company to the Channel Islands. In 2001 the company started a joint ferry service with Brittany Ferries using the ***Condor Vitesse*** to Cherbourg. The route has proved successful as a fast ferry operation for both operators and will be repeated in 2003.
(John Hendy)

Above: Truckline Ferries were the original company to put Poole on the map as a Channel port. Poole offered the closest link between Britain and Normandy and the freight dedicated company was to blossom from the port until its takeover by Brittany Ferries. Today, the ***Coutances***, sister to the ***Purbeck*** illustrated on page 31, is employed to run the service. The vessel is supported by the ro-pax vessel ***Barfleur*** which entered service on the route initially as a Truckline vessel in 1992 but latterly marketed as Brittany Ferries service as from 1999. The vessel is able to accommodate 550 cars and 1,173 passengers on the four hour link between both ports. *(John Bryant)*

ondor Express is seen leaving St. Helier, Jersey on her morning crossing from Poole. Condor not only use Poole as their UK port but also Weymouth on certain scheduled s. The reliability of both the ***Condor Express*** and ***Condor Vitesse*** has improved remarkably in recent years and with the support of the ro-pax vessel ***Commodore Clipper,*** ers have been given a far more reliable service.The picture takes in the ***Commodore Goodwill*** which is also seen underway for Portsmouth. *(Miles Cowsill)*

CHANNEL ISLANDS

Above: The ***Condor 10*** arrives at St Helier from St Malo to take up summer runs between the Channel Islands and France. *(Miles Cowsill)*

Below: The ferry service between St. Malo and St. Helier is operated by Emeraude Lines of France. Currently the company have two catamaran vessels which are able to carry cars and passengers. The newer of them, ***Solidor 5***, introduced in January 2001, is able to take 60 cars and 450 passengers and maintains the St. Malo-St Helier route on a year round basis. The older craft, the ***Solidor 4***, operates in tandem with the ***Solidor 5*** during the summer period. *(Miles Cowsill)*

Top Right: The Island of Sark is served by Sark Shipping Company, who are responsible for ensuring that the Islanders are supplied with food and materials for their daily life plus during the summer season regular day trips to the Island for tourists. In recent years the company has had to reduce its fleet with the decline of holidaymakers visiting this picturesque Island. The ***Bon Marin de Serk*** (seen here) departs on a July morning pleasure sailing to the Island. *(John Hendy)*

Left: The ***Herm Clipper*** loads at St. Peter Port for her short passage across the Little Russel to Herm. *(John Hendy)*

Below: Travel Trident also operate ferry services to the Island of Herm and one of their craft, the ***Trident V***, is seen here loading at St. Peter Port. *(John Hendy)*

Above: British Channel Island Ferries' ***Rozel*** (ex ***St. Edmund*** and ***Scirocco***) arrives at Poole from the Channel Islands in the company's final year of operations in 1993. The vessel was to be the largest ever ship on the Channel Islands' links from the UK. Today she is employed on a ferry link between Spain and Morocco. *(Miles Cowsill)*

Below: The ***Earl William*** is seen here at St. Peter Port following her morning arrival from St. Helier during her final season on the Channel Islands' services. The vessel was to have an interesting career after leaving the English Channel services, including further operations within the Sealink fleet on the Irish Sea. At one stage the vessel was chartered by the Government as a prison ship and today she still remains in service on the Adriatic, but with an uncertain future. *(Miles Cowsill)*

PLYMOUTH-ROSCOFF

Above: This view shows Brittany Ferries' ***Tregastel*** in her original guise whilst on the Roscoff-Plymouth service. On the entry into service of the ***Bretagne*** the vessel was sold to P&O Scottish Ferries and renamed ***St. Clair***. The Yugoslavian-built ship is pictured on page 2 in her later career with P&O. *(Miles Cowsill)*

Below: In 1992 Brittany Ferries purchased from TT Line the ***Nils Holgersson*** which had originally been built for their Travemunde-Trelleborg operation. After extensive rebuilding, she entered service as the ***Val de Loire*** in Spring 1993 to maintain the Plymouth-Santander, Roscoff-Cork and Roscoff-Plymouth operations. Since her introduction into the Brittany Ferries fleet she has maintained the Spanish and Irish services during the summer and during the winter period has supported the Caen service when the Spanish and Irish services are not operated. The ship has also been utilised for a number of one off cruises during the Christmas and New Year periods and has visited many interesting ports including Amsterdam and Rouen. It seems likely that she will transfer to the St Malo route in 2004. *(Miles Cowsill)*

Brittany Ferries

The ***Quiberon*** until recently was the oldest vessel in the Brittany Ferries fleet and has been a reliable workhorse for the company since her introduction in 1984. Originally built as the ***Nils Dacke*** the vessel is a sister ship to the ***Norrona*** operated by Smyril Line (see page 109). The ***Quiberon*** was replaced on the Roscoff operation by the ***Duc de Normandie*** in July 2002. The vessel completed her career with the French company during the latter part of 2002 on the Caen service. *(Miles Cowsill)*

WEST COUNTRY

Above: Three large chain ferries maintain the busy Torpoint Ferry service linking Torpoint in Cornwall with Devonport (Plymouth) across the River Tamar. They each carry 350 passengers and about 50 cars and the newest vessel, the ***Plym*** of 1968 is seen above loading at Devonport. Three higher capacity ferries are expected to replace the present vessels in 2003. *(John Hendy)*

Below: The new Fowey-Bodinnick ferry ***Jenack*** entered service in 2000 and is seen about to leave Fowey on her five minute trip. She carries 48 passengers and 9 cars. *(John Hendy)*

Above: The Dart Higher Ferry is operated by a cable-guided, paddle driven vessel built in 1960 and capable of accommodating 136 passengers and 18 cars on the five minute crossing. She is seen ready to leave the Dartmouth side in July 2002. *(John Hendy)*

Below: The Lower Dart Ferry is operated between Dartmouth and Kingswear by the South Hams District Council. The service is maintained by twin floats called ***The Tom Avis*** and ***The Tom Casey*** which are manoeuvred by the tugs ***Hauley V*** and ***Hauley VI***. *(John Hendy)*

Above: The present King Harry Ferry dates from 1974 and accommodates 100 passengers and 28 cars on this most picturesque of British ferry crossings, across the upper reaches of the River Fal. *(John Hendy)*

Below: The ***Scillonian III*** is owned and operated by the Isles of Scilly Steamship Company. She was built in 1977 for the 2 hour 40 minute Penzance - St. Mary's run and is the last conventional passenger-only ferry in service within the UK. Her sturdy hull form speaks volumes for the nature of the link that the vessel maintains. *(Adrian Symons)*

The ***Isle of Innisfree*** sails through the calm waters of Milford Haven on her way to Pembroke Dock. The introduction of the ship on the Rosslare route was to revive its fortunes and bring about serious doubts concerning the future of the rival Fishguard link. *(Miles Cowsill)*

SWANSEA & PEMBROKE DOCK

Left: Following the demise of B&I's operations between Swansea and Cork, a new service was established by Swansea Cork Ferries in 1987. The company has had a variety of ferries on the service over the years. The vessel which has possibly been the most successful has been the ***Superferry*** from Strintzis Lines of Greece. In 2001 the company acquired the vessel from the Greek company. They have employed a variety of nationalities onboard their ships over the years in an effort to save costs and to make the route profitable against their rivals further along the coast at Pembroke Dock and Fishguard. The ***Superferry*** pictured here as the ***Blue Aegean*** is seen at Piraeus in 2001 whilst operating in Greek waters when the company were unable to charter her for their summer operations. *(Miles Cowsill)*

Above: In 1980 B&I Line opened a rival ferry service to Sealink at Fishguard between Rosslare and Pembroke Dock. The route was initially opened by the ***Viking III*** in 1980 and a series of unsuitable vessels were to follow her during the 80s and 90s as the state-owned company were unable to invest in suitable tonnage for the route. On privatisation of the nationalised company Irish Ferries invested in the route and its fortunes have dramatically turned around. Today the route is operated by the giant ***Isle of Inishmore,*** originally built for the Dublin-Holyhead route. The success of Irish Ferries at Pembroke Dock may in the future see the demise of Stena Line's operations at Fishguard. *(Miles Cowsill)*

FISHGUARD

Above: The port of Fishguard has everything a ferry port should have, a railway line, good road communications on the A40 to the M4 and a fully operational port at all tides. Since the port was opened in 1907 it has flourished but in recent years under the ownership of Stena Line the port has become less economic. Today the route is maintained by the ***Stena Europe*** and in addition during the summer period the ***Stena Lynx III***. *(Gordon Hislip)*

Right: The ***Normandy*** leaves Pembroke Dock for Rosslare whilst covering for the ***Isle of Inishmore***. The ***Normandy*** is employed in the Irish Ferries fleet to maintain their Rosslare-Cherbourg/Roscoff link which competes with that of Brittany Ferries. She is the sister to the ***Stena Europe***. *(Miles Cowsill)*

KONINGIN BEATRIX

The ***Koningin Beatrix*** was transferred from the Harwich-Hook of Holland service to the Fishguard-Rosslare route in 1997. Whilst the vessel brought improved standards to the Irish Sea, she was never really suitable for the service with such a high capacity of cabins onboard. Stena Line transferred the ship to their Polish service in March 2002 and renamed her ***Stena Baltica.*** *(Miles Cowsill)*

HOLYHEAD

Right: Stena Line chartered the Italian ro-pax vessel the ***Stena Forwarder*** in 2001. She is seen here approaching the port of Dublin inward from Holyhead. Operationally the ship has proved difficult to handle at both ports but has proved successful for the Swedish company in offering extra capacity for freight on the Central Corridor. The ***Stena Forwarder*** replaced the ***Stena Challenger*** which now operates in Canadian waters. *(Miles Cowsill)*

Below: The Central Corridor of the Irish Sea has very much become the core of operations between the UK and Ireland. Both Irish Ferries and Stena Line in an effort to attract customers to their operations have introduced a variety of different tonnage in recent years. In 1996 the Swedish company Stena Line introduced the revolutionary HSS craft the ***Stena Explorer*** which was able to carry passengers cars and freight at a speed of 40 knots. Whilst the craft has proved successful to meet a gap in their operations with the older tonnage inherited from Sealink, her operating costs have been their downfall with the escalation of fuel prices in recent years. In 2001 Irish Ferries introduced the world's largest capacity ferry the ***Ulysses*** which has proved successful for the company. Both rival ships are seen approaching the pier at Holyhead. *(Miles Cowsill)*

STENA FORWARDER
Stena Line
STENA FORWARDER
BARI

Stena Line
HSS
Stena Line

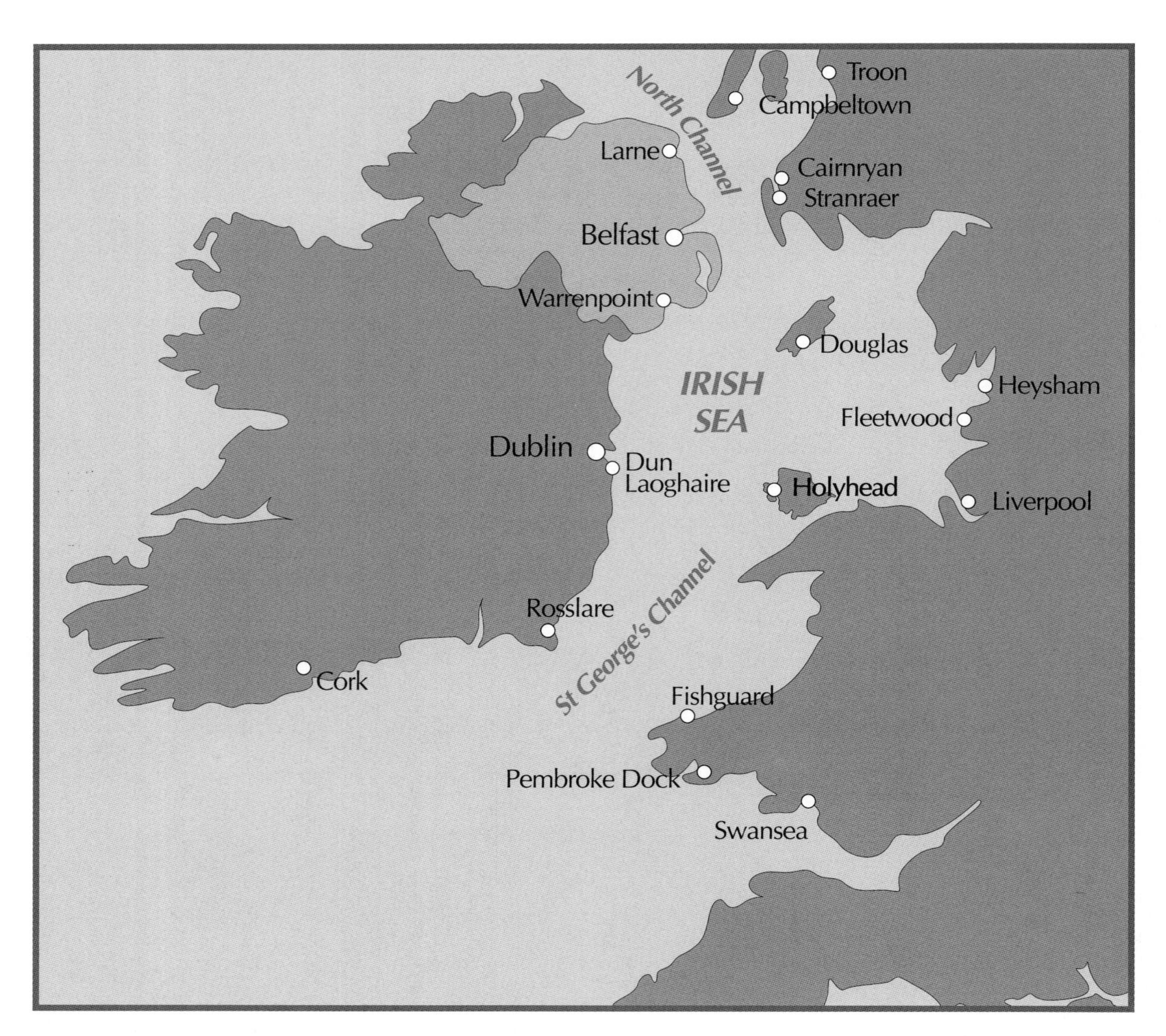

Above: Irish Ferries operate the Austal-built craft the ***Jonathan Swift*** in tandem with the giant ***Ulysses***. This craft can maintain a service speed of 35.5 knots and can carry up to 200 cars and 800 passengers. She is a sister to the ***SuperStar Express*** which operates for P&O Irish Sea on the Cairnryan-Larne route (see page 81). *(Miles Cowsill)*

Above: Another view of the ***Ulysses*** outward bound from Dublin to Holyhead. *(Miles Cowsill)*

Below: The giant HSS ***Stena Explorer*** manoeuvres into the port of Holyhead from Dun Laoghaire. HSS craft in the fleet of Stena Line currently operate between Stranraer and Belfast, Harwich and the Hook of Holland and Holyhead-Dun Laoghaire. The three vessels built to date cannot be moved to other ports as they have to be supported by dedicated infrastructure at each end of the operation. *(Miles Cowsill)*

Above: Following the introduction of the HSS between Holyhead and Dublin, the former ***Stena Hibernia*** was renamed ***Stena Adventurer*** as a back-up vessel on the link. The vessel, originally built as the ***St. Columba*** in Denmark, is seen here during her last season on the Irish Sea. Today she operates for Hellas Ferries as the ***Express Aphrodite***. *(Miles Cowsill)*

Below: The ***Stena Cambria*** was built originally as the ***St. Anselm*** for the Dover-Calais route. She is seen following her transfer from Folkestone arriving at Dun Laoghaire. Today she is employed on a ferry service between Barcelona and Ibiza and renamed the ***Isla de Botafoc***. *(Miles Cowsill)*

HOLYHEAD & LIVERPOOL

Top Right: In late 2001 P&O Irish Sea inaugurated a new ferry link from the Welsh port of Mostyn to Dublin using the ***European Ambassador*** and the ***European Envoy***, which had previously been employed on the Liverpool service. The ***European Ambassador*** is pictured alongside prior to her morning sailing from Dublin. *(Miles Cowsill)*

Right: During 2001 P&O Irish Sea commenced an experimental service using the chartered ***Celtic Star*** (renamed ***Northern Star*** in January 2002) between Liverpool and Larne. The service was discontinued in December when the charter of the Japanese-built ship ceased. The vessel is seen arriving at Larne during August. *(John Hendy)*

Below: In a surprise move in 2002, P&O Irish Sea chartered from their parent company P&O North Sea Ferries the ***Norbank*** and ***Norbay*** (pictured here) to maintain their Liverpool-Dublin service. These vessels may in the future be transferred to the Mostyn link as they would provide a three sailings a day service from both ports with their excellent service speed. *(Miles Cowsill)*

LIVERPOOL

Above: In 2002 the ***SuperSeaCat Three*** carried out a triangle service for Sea Containers' operations on the Irish Sea. The vessel was employed in the mornings to run between Liverpool and Dublin and in the early evening ran an additional sailing for the Isle of Man Steam Packet to Douglas. She is seen at the Landing Stage with the magnificent Royal Liver Building behind her. *(John Hendy)*

Below Left: The ***Dawn Merchant*** arrives at Dublin from Liverpool. The vessel has been transferred to the Dover-Dunkirk service of Norfolkline since this view was taken in May 2002. *(Miles Cowsill)*

Below: The Mersey ferries have been very much an integral part of life and also a vital service for residents of both Liverpool Wallasey and Birkenhead. This view shows the ***Woodchurch*** on her regular triangular service from Wallasey and Birkenhead to the Landing Stage. The vessel dates back to 1960 and is able to carry 750 passengers. *(John Hendy)*

FLEETWOOD & HEYSHAM

Above: In 1999 Norse Merchant Ferries chartered the Spanish-built ***Varbola***. The Estonian vessel is pictured inward bound to Dublin from Heysham in May 2002. *(Miles Cowsill)*

Left: SeaTruck Ferries operate a dedicated service between Heysham and Warrenpoint in Northern Ireland. Two ships are currently employed on the route, the ***Moondance*** and ***Riverdance***. The ***Monedance*** is seen here leaving Warrenpoint outward bound for Heysham. *(Ferries Publications Library)*

Below: The 12 passenger Knott End ferry ***Princess Anne*** on the beach at Fleetwood. There are hopes for the long-term future of the service using something rather more substantial than this converted fishing boat. *(John Hendy)*

ISLE OF MAN

Right: This historic view shows the ro-ro vessel ***Peveril*** in her last year of operation with the Isle of Man Steam Packet Company. The picture includes the ***SeaCat Isle of Man*** pending her afternoon departure to Dublin. The SeaCat service has brought improved summer operations for the islanders since its introduction in 1994 but the company is still forced during the winter periods to maintain a conventional service with the ***Lady of Mann***. *(Miles Cowsill)*

Below: The ***Ben-my-Chree*** comes astern onto the berth at Douglas on her evening arrival at the port from Heysham. The ***Lady of Mann*** is alongside on Victoria Pier pending her early evening sailing to Heysham during the TT period in 2002. *(Miles Cowsill)*

The ***King Orry*** arrives at Douglas in her last few weeks in service prior to the entry into service of the new ro-pax vessel ***Ben-my-Chree***. The vessel today operates for Moby Lines as the ***Moby Love II***. Originally she was built as the ***Saint Eloi*** for the Dunkirk-Dover train ferry service. *(Miles Cowsill)*

BELFAST

Above: The ***Lagan Viking*** leaves Liverpool on her day crossing to Belfast. This Italian-built vessel is able to carry 340 passengers and 100 cars and operates in tandem with the ***Mersey Viking*** from the new Twelve Quays River Terminal at Birkenhead. *(John Hendy)*

Below: The ***River Lune*** was built in Romania in the series of ships known as the Bazias C\lass. She is employed today by Norse Merchant Ferries on their Heysham-Belfast route. The vessel is pictured arriving in Dublin Bay from the Lancashire port. *(John Hendy)*

Right: The ***Rapide*** arrives at Belfast from Heysham. The vessel was originally the ***Condor 12*** and then later became the ***Holyman Rapide*** when she inaugurated the Ramsgate-Ostend service in 1997. During 2001 the vessel was employed on the Liverpool-Dublin/Douglas service and in 2002 was introduced on the Heysham-Belfast service to offer additional capacity on the route. Due to major technical problems, the seasonal service had to be suspended early in 2002. For 2003 she is due to run on the Belfast-Troon service. *(Miles Cowsill)*

Right: The ***SeaCat Scotland*** pulls away from Troon on her crossing to Belfast in August 2002. Of all the InCat craft purchased by Sea Containers, the ***SeaCat Scotland***, has spent most of her career on the Irish Sea, apart from a short charter in 1997 in South America and a brief spell at Dover. In late 2002 the vessel was withdrawn from service and offered for sale; she was replaced by ***SeaCat Isle of Man*** during the winter period of 2002/2003. *(John Hendy)*

Below: The HSS ***Stena Voyager*** picks up speed off the entrance of Loch Ryan en route to Belfast. Currently Stena Line's operations between Stranraer and Belfast are maintained by the HSS craft and the ***Stena Caledonia***. *(John Hendy)*

LARNE

Above: The ***European Endeavour*** was built as the ***European Enterprise*** for the Dover-Zeebrugge service. In 1995 she was transferred to the Irish Sea. The attractive freight vessel is seen approaching Larne in May 2002 during her last couple of weeks in service with P&O. She was subsequently sold to TransEuropa for service between Ramsgate and Ostend and renamed ***Gardenia.*** *(Miles Cowsill)*

Left: P&O Irish Sea introduced the ***European Causeway*** in 2000 as part of a rapid expansion of the group and major multi-million pound investment in new tonnage on the Irish Sea. The vessel is seen arriving at Larne. She was joined in July 2002 by an identical sister, the ***European Highlander.*** Both ships are now the mainstay of the Larne-Cairnryan service. *(Miles Cowsill)*

Left: The ***European Navigator*** (ex ***Viking Trader***) is pictured arriving at Larne from Cairnryan. The vessel was originally built in Austria as the ***Stena Trader*** and has had an interesting career with numerous companies worldwide. During her career with P&O she has carried the name ***Viking Trader***, ***Leopard*** and in 1988 renamed the ***European Navigator*** in line with the rest of the fleet within the P&O Group.In Summer 2002 she served on the Larne-Troon link. *(John Hendy)*

Right: The ***SuperStar Express*** has successfully operated on the North Channel since April 2000 and currently operates in tandem with the conventional ships during the summer period. The vessel was employed earlier in her career by P&O Portsmouth to open their new fast ferry service between Portsmouth and Cherbourg.
(John Hendy)

Below: P&O Irish Sea not only operates to Cairnryan in Scotland from Larne but also to the port of Troon. This dedicated freight service in recent years has become a more important operation for the company. The current vessel on the service, the ***European Mariner***, is pictured at Portsmouth whilst on charter to Commodore in September 2002, prior to return to the Larne - Troon service in place of the ***European Navigator***.
(Miles Cowsill)

LARNE & STRANRAER

Above: The ***Ailsa Princess*** was built for the Stranraer-Larne service in 1971. In 1982 she was transferred to the Weymouth-Cherbourg service and some three years later renamed ***Earl Harold***. Following her withdrawal from the Sealink fleet in 1989, she was sold to GA Ferries and renamed ***Dimitra.*** In 1994 she was sold to Agapitos Lines and renamed ***Naias Express***. Following the absorption of her owners into Hellas Ferries she currently carries the name ***Express Adonis***. *(FotoFlite)*

Left: The ***Stena Caledonia*** (ex ***St. David***) was originally planned to replace the ***Stena Normandica*** on the Fishguard-Rosslare service. In the event the last of the Saint vessels was placed on the Holyhead-Dun Laoghaire route. The vessel had an interesting career whilst operating for Sealink, including opening a new ferry service for the company with RMT between Dover and Ostend. The vessel remains in service today as the ***Stena Caledonia*** on the Stranraer-Belfast service in tandem with the ***Stena Voyager***. The vessel is pictured here leaving Larne in Stena Sealink livery. *(Miles Cowsill)*

Right:: The ***SeaCat Scotland*** was the fifth 74 metre catamaran to be built by InCat in Australia. In 1992 she inaugurated a new high speed service between Stranraer and Belfast. She is seen here during her first season arriving in Belfast Lough. *(Ferry Publications Library)*

Below: The ***Europic Ferry*** was to play an important and integral part in the expansion of Townsend Thoresen's operations on the North Channel. The ***Europic Ferry*** has the important accolade of also being involved in the recapture of the Falkland Islands in 1982. Today she is owned by Med Link Lines and sails between Brindisi and Patras in Greece as the **Afrodite II**. *(Ferry Publications Library)*

Scotland

THE CLYDE

Left: The ***Caledonian Isles*** was built in 1993 for Caledonian MacBrayne in the light of demands for increased capacity on the Ardrossan-Brodick (Arran) service. Since her introduction she has maintained the 55 minute service to Arran. *(Miles Cowsill)*

Below: The ***Juno***, ***Jupiter*** (pictured here)and ***Saturn*** were built for the Gourock-Dunoon, Gourock-Kilcreggan and Wemyss Bay-Rothesay services. The vessels are now nearly 30 years old and are due for replacement in the near future. The ***Jupiter*** was upgraded to Class III standard to enable her to stand in on the Ardrossan-Brodick service. Before 1986, the ***Juno*** and the ***Jupiter*** operated mainly on the Gourock-Dunoon and Gourock-Kilcreggan services and the ***Saturn*** on the Wemyss Bay-Rothesay service. Since 1986 they have usually been rotated on a three-weekly basis on the three services. *(Miles Cowsill)*

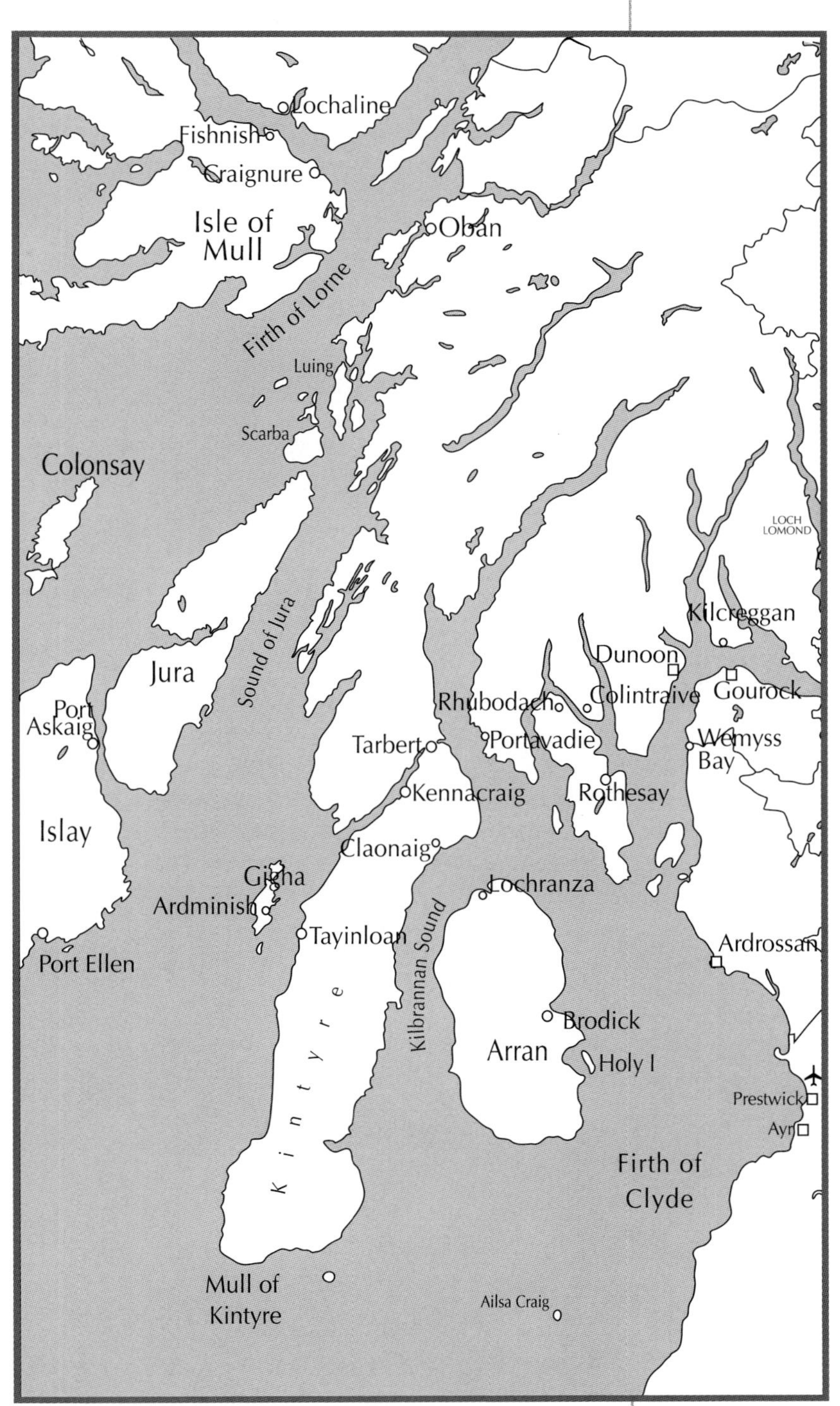

Below: The ***Isle of Cumbrae*** was originally built for the Largs-Cumbrae operation in 1977. Some nine years later she was replaced on this service and transferred to the Lochaline-Fishnish (Mull) service. In 1997 she was placed on the Colintraive-Rhubodach link. Two years later she was transferred to the Tarbert-Portavadie service. She is seen here at Tarbert in 2001. *(Miles Cowsill)*

Below: The ***Loch Tarbert*** approaches a peaceful Lochranza (Arran). Very much the second link to Arran, but possibly one of the prettiest on the Clyde. Kintyre lies in the distance. *(Miles Cowsill)*

Above: The ***Pioneer*** was built at Leith to operate the West Loch Tarbert-Port Ellen service. She was latterly transferred to the Mallaig-Armadale service in 1978 and also sailed as relief vessel on the Clyde. Since 1995 she has been employed mainly on the Clyde and she is seen here arriving off Wemyss Bay. *(Miles Cowsill)*

Below: The ***Loch Dunvegan*** was constructed for the Kyle of Lochalsh-Kyleakin service prior to the completion of the Skye Bridge. In October 1995 she was withdrawn from service and offered for sale by Caledonian MacBrayne. In the event she was not sold and currently operates between Colintraive and Rhubodach. *(Miles Cowsill)*

JUPITER

This wonderful view of the Clyde takes in the ***Jupiter*** inward bound to Rothesay. *(Miles Cowsill)*

Above: Looking over the car deck of the ***Saturn*** as she leaves the port of Rothesay. The ***Juno***, ***Jupiter*** and ***Saturn*** are able to unload cars both on the port and starboard side and also at the stern, depending upon the port facilities on the Clyde. *(Miles Cowsill)*

Left: The ***Sound of Sleat*** was built in the Netherlands for the ferry service between Maassluis and Rozenburg, across the New Waterway in the Netherlands. In 1988 she was purchased by Western Ferries and remains an integral part of the fleet. *(Brian Maxted)*

Right: The ***Sound of Scarba*** was built in 2001 for the services of Western Ferries between Hunter's Quay and McInroy's Point. This vessel is able to accommodate 220 passengers and 40 cars on the 20 minute service. *(Brian Maxted)*

Below: The ***Sound of Shuna*** was built in Sweden as the ***Ölandssund IV*** to sail between Revsudden on mainland Sweden and the Island of Öland. Following the opening of a bridge linking the island, the ferry service ceased. In 1973 she was sold with her near sister the ***Sound of Scarba***. Currently the ***Sound of Shuna*** is the reserve vessel in the Western Ferries' fleet. *(Brian Maxted)*

WESTERN ISLES

Above: Argyll and Bute Council are responsible for is the five minute service between Seil and Luing. The vessel employed on this route is the ***Belnahua*** and she is able to carry five cars and 40 passengers. The vessel runs an infrequent service, depending upon demand. (*Miles Cowsill)*

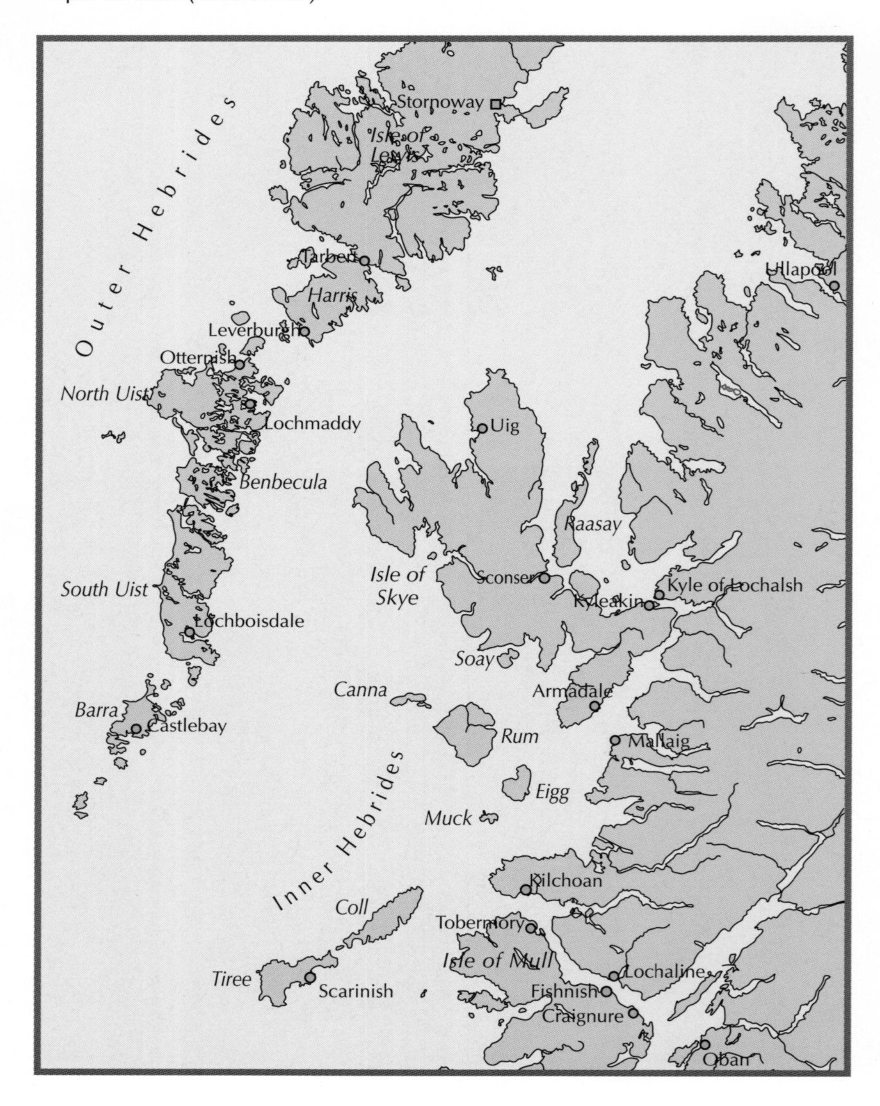

The Argyll and Bute Council ferry the ***Eilean Dhiura*** maintains a regular service between the islands of Islay and Jura. She is seen here arriving off Islay on her last round crossing of the day. The service is not only vital to residents of the island of Jura but also to the distillery on the island. (*Miles Cowsill)*

Above: The ***Isle of Mull*** is the mainstay of the Oban-Craignure service. She is able to carry some 80 cars and 962 passengers. The popularity of Mull as a tourist destination and increased demand from the residents of the Island may see a larger vessel being introduced in the near future. *(Miles Cowsill)*

Right: One of the smallest ships in the Caledonian MacBrayne fleet is the ***Eigg***. She is seen here outward bound from Oban to Lismore. She is able to carry only 6 cars and dates back to 1975. *(Miles Cowsill)*

Below: The ***Hebridean Isles*** leaves Oban on her first sailing from the resort to Colonsay in April 2001. *(Miles Cowsill)*

Caledonian MacBrayne
ANTIC LIMITED
CARRIER
CLANSMAN
GLASGOW

Above: The ***Clansman*** has a fairly intensive timetable throughout the year as she is responsible for maintaining links to the Islands of Barra, South Uist, Coll and Tiree. The vessel is seen here departing from Oban for Castlebay and Lochboisdale. *(Miles Cowsill)*

Below: The ***Isle of Arran*** is now the relief vessel with the Caledonian MacBrayne fleet. The vessel is seen, with the Paps of Jura behind, arriving at Port Askaig (Islay) from Oban. *(Miles Cowsill)*

Above: The ***Lochnevis*** was built to replace the ***Lochmor*** on the Small Isles service from Mallaig. Although a vehicle ferry, cars are not normally carried to the islands of Eigg, Muck and Rum as this facility is usually used to carry agricultural machinery and livestock. The vessel is seen here arriving at Mallaig during her second year in service. *(Miles Cowsill)*

Below: Possibly one of the most attractive looking vessels built in recent years for Caledonian MacBrayne is the ***Lord of the Isles***. Currently the vessel has been employed to operate during the summer between Mallaig and Armadale and also from Mallaig to the Outer Isles. As from 2003 the ***Lord of the Isles*** will be based at Oban and she will no longer run from Mallaig to Barra and South Uist. The vessel is seen outward bound to Mallaig in April 2001 in wintry conditions. *(Miles Cowsill)*

Right: A late evening scene as the ***Loch Striven*** arrives at the linkspan on Skye from Raasay. The vessel possibly has one of the easiest operations within the Caledonian MacBrayne fleet today. *(Miles Cowsill)*

Below: The newest vessel in the fleet of Caledonian MacBrayne is the ***Hebrides***. The vessel is seen here inward bound from North Uist arriving at Uig on Skye. *(Miles Cowsill)*

Left: A vital link between the islands of North Uist and Harris has been maintained by the ***Loch Bhrusda***. She will be replaced by the new ***Loch Portain*** in 2003 and transferred to a new Caledonian MacBrayne route between Eriskay and Barra. She is seen here inward bound to Otternish on North Uist. *(Miles Cowsill)*

Right: The Highlands Council maintain the ferry service between Corran and Ardgour. This five minute passage offers a vital link across the loch for both motorists and locals. The ***Corran*** is seen here unloading at her namesake on Loch Linnhe near Fort William. *(Andrew Cooke)*

Below: The ***Isle of Lewis*** currently maintains the busy ferry link between Ullapool and Stornoway. In recent years there has not only been an increase in passenger traffic but also a substantial rise in freight traffic from the Islands to the mainland of Scotland with the expansion of fish farming on Lewis and Harris. *(Colin Smith)*

Caledonian MacBrayne
LOCH FYNE

Left: The ***Loch Fyne*** makes for Kyle of Lochalsh with the partly completed Skye Bridge and mountains of Skye as a backdrop during May 1995. *(Colin Smith).*

Below Left: The magnificent former David MacBrayne turbine steamer ***King George V*** pictured in Caledonian MacBrayne livery at anchor off Iona on one of her regular round Mull excursions in 1973. One of MacBrayne's 'red boats' is tendering to her. *(John Hendy)*

Below: The ***Iona*** arrives at Mallaig during her last season on the Skye service. Today she operates as the ***Pentalina B*** between Gills Bay and Orkney. *(Miles Cowsill)*

ORKNEY & SHETLAND

Above: The ***Hoy Head*** arrives at Lyness on Hoy. This vessel is able to carry 125 passengers and 18 cars and was built at Bideford in England to replace the ***Thorsvoe*** which now is the reserve vessel in the Orkney Ferries fleet. *(Willie Mackay)*

Below: The ***Graemsay*** and the ***Golden Mariana*** are pictured together in this view at Stromness shortly after their refits. *(Willie Mackay)*

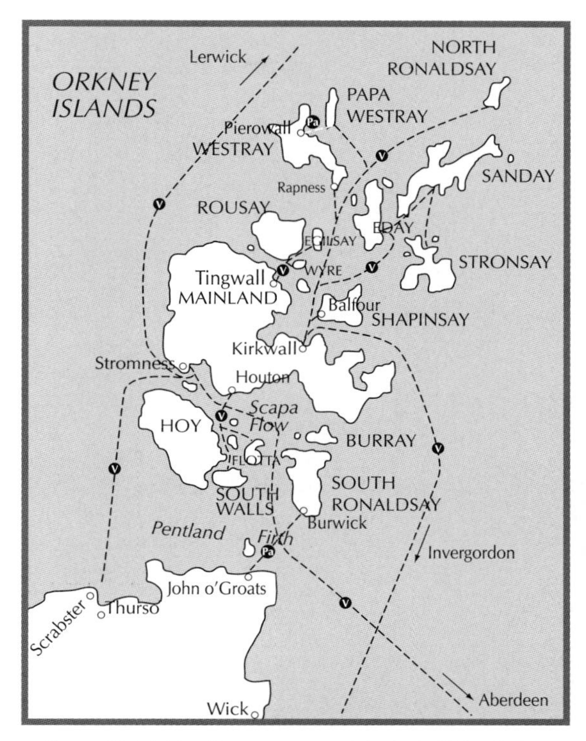

Above Right: The ***Varagen*** was originally built to start a new service between Gills Bay (Caithness, Scotland) and Burwick (South Ronaldsay, Orkney). However, due to problems with the terminals, it was not possible for her to maintain a regular service and eventually the vessel was transferred to operate the North Isles services with the ***Earl Sigurd*** and the ***Earl Thorfinn***. *(Nicholas Meads)*

Below: The ***Shapinsay*** is pictured here outward bound from Kirkwall. The vessel is employed on the Shapinsay service and is one of the smallest vessels in the company's fleet. *(Anthony Meads)*

Above: A wonderful view over the town of Stromness takes in the ***St. Sunniva*** as she arrives from Aberdeen. In the background can be seen Scapa Flow and the islands of Burray and South Ronaldsay. She has been sold for further service and has been renamed the ***Faye***. *(Willie Mackay)*

Left: The ***St. Ola*** is pictured here leaving Stromness during her penultimate season on the Pentland Firth service. Her replacement, the ***Hamnavoe,*** will be able to carry 600 passengers and 95 cars. *(Willie Mackay)*

Above : The ***Pentland Venture*** operates a summer only passenger service linking John o'Groats with Burwick (South Ronaldsay). (*Anthony Meads)*

Below: Shetland Ferries' ***Linga*** at Laxo on the Whalsay service. This vessel built in Poland is able to carry 100 passengers and 16 cars. (*Andrew Cooke)*

Passengers and cars arrive at Lerwick's Bressay Ferry Terminal as the *Grima* starts to unload her traffic. *(Andrew Cooke)*

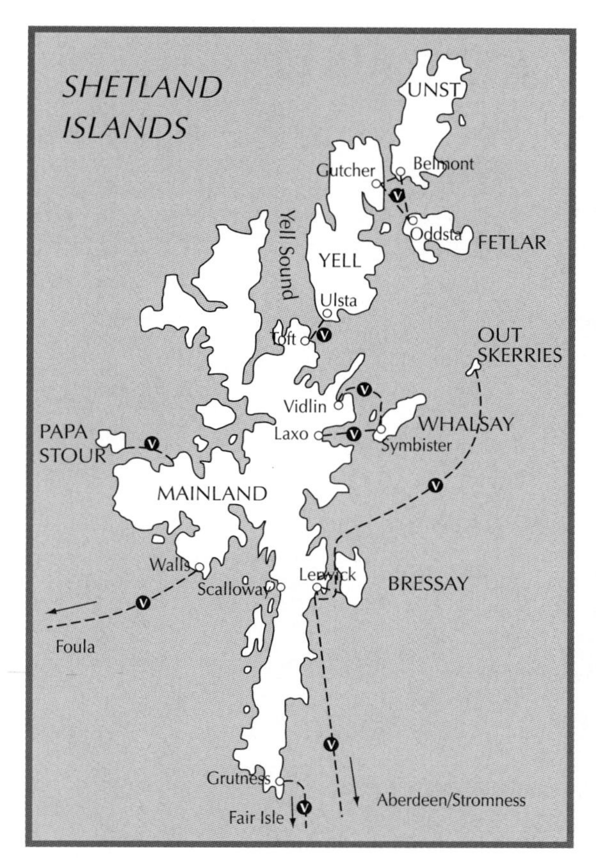

Right: The ***Bigga*** makes an impressive view as she approaches Ulsta (Yell). The vessel since her construction in 1991 has maintained the 20 minute Toft-Ulsta service. *(Miles Cowsill)*

Below: The ***St. Clair*** outward bound from Lerwick to Aberdeen in her last few weeks in service with P&O Scottish Ferries before the takeover of the route by NorthLink Ferries. *(Andrew Cooke)*

Above: The ***St. Rognvald*** and the ***St. Sunniva*** at their layover at the port of Lerwick. Both vessels have recently been disposed of by P&O Scottish Ferries following the company losing the contractual rights to operate between mainland Scotland, Shetland and Orkney. *(Miles Cowsill)*

Top Left: A blustery spring scene as the ***Leirna*** arrives at Lerwick. Since this vessel was introduced by Shetland Islands Council in 1992 she has maintained the Bressay service. *(Miles Cowsill)*

Left: The ***Thora*** was built in the Faroe Islands. She was withdrawn from service in 2001 and now is the spare vessel in the Council's fleet. Her sisters, the ***Fylga*** and the ***Grima***, are also due to be replaced in the near future. *(Miles Cowsill)*

Right: The ***Norrona***, sister to Brittany Ferries' ***Quiberon***, has been a regular visitor to the Shetland Islands. Smyril Line are due to replace her in 2003 with a larger vessel which will be able to accommodate 1,482 passengers and 800 cars. The vessel is seen here at Bergen pending her departure to Lerwick. *(Willie Mackay)*

P&O
P&O
St Sunniva

SMYRIL-LINE
NORRÖNA
TÓRSHAVN

Left: This interesting view shows the ***Good Shepherd IV*** unloading a van at Grutness. The vessel is employed and operated from Grutness to Fair Isle. Vehicles are carried on this vessel by special arrangement and generally consist of agricultural vehicles. The vessel is pulled up on a marine slip on Fair Isle at the conclusion of each voyage. *(Brian Maxted)*

Below: The ***Fivla*** leaves the island of Unst for Gutcher on Yell. This vessel was built in Troon in 1985 and is able to accommodate 95 passengers and 15 cars. *(Brian Maxted)*

Above: The ***Hjaltland*** (pictured here) with her sister the ***Hrossey*** now maintain the Orkney and Shetland Isles services of NorthLink Ferries. *(NorthLink Ferries)*

Right: The new NorthLink Ferries vessel ***Hamnavoe*** is pictured here at the Ocean Terminal at Leith pending entry into service from Scrabster. This picture also takes in the ***Faye*** (ex P&O Scottish Ferries' vessel ***St. Sunniva***) ahead of her departure to her new owners. *(Colin Smith)*

East coast of Britain

NORTH SEA

Above: The ***Superfast X*** comes astern from Zeebrugge port en route to Rosyth. The ***Superfast X*** and her sister the ***Superfast IX*** which were built in Germany have an impressive operational speed of 29.2 knots and can maintain the Zeebrugge-Rosyth service in 16 hours. *(Barry Mitchell)*

Left: North Sea Ferries maintain the freight-only service between Middlesbrough and Zeebrugge using the giant chartered ro-ro vessels ***Norqueen*** and ***Norking.*** The ***Norqueen*** is seen here at Rotterdam whilst covering a refit period. *(Miles Cowsill)*

Right: Fjord Line's veteran ***Jupiter*** arrives at North Shields from Bergen. The ***Jupiter*** was originally built as the ***Wellamo*** in 1975 and some six years later was sold to DFDS and renamed the ***Dana Gloria***. During the winter of 1988/89 she was lengthened in Germany and renamed the ***King of Scandinavia*** for the company's Copenhagen-Oslo route. In 1994 she was sold to Color Line and renamed ***Color Viking***. Following the takeover in 1998 of the route, Fjord Line renamed her the ***Jupiter.*** *(Matthew Punter)*

Above: The ***Prince of Scandinavia*** and ***Princess of Scandinavia*** were built in the mid-seventies and have been very much part of the scene at both Harwich and Newcastle since their construction. Today the ***Princess of Scandinavia*** maintains the Norwegian/Swedish service from the UK whilst her sister, the ***Prince of Scandinavia***, operates between Newcastle and IJmuiden. The 'Prince' is pictured here prior to her modification with the fitting of sponsons. *(FotoFlite)*

Left: The ***Queen of Scandinavia*** is seen here at IJmuiden. The vessel was transferred from Scandinavia in 2001 to offer additional capacity on DFDS Seaways' North Sea ferry service to Holland. *(John van der Linden)*

Above: The ***Admiral of Scandinavia*** was built as the ***Kronprins Harald*** for Jahre Line of Norway. In 1987 she was purchased by DFDS and renamed ***Hamburg*** for their Harwich-Hamburg service. In 1997 she was transferred to the Newcastle-IJmuiden/Hamburg operation and renamed ***Admiral of Scandinavia***. In October 2002 she was sold by DFDS for further service in the Caribbean. *(John Hendy)*

Below: The ***Pride of Hull*** and ***Pride of Rotterdam*** were built in Italy for P&O North Sea Ferries for their Hull-Europort service. The British-registered vessel is pictured here inward bound from the UK during her first season in service on the link. *(Rob de Visser)*

Above: The ***Norstar*** (pictured here) and the ***Norland*** were originally built for the Hull-Europort service. On the introduction of larger tonnage in the late eighties on the Europort service, they were transferred to the Zeebrugge route. The ***Norland*** has the distinction of being a Falkland Islands veteran and played an important part in the conflict conveying troops to the Islands. Both vessels have recently been sold for further service in Italy. *(John Hendy)*

Below: The British registered ***Norsea*** is captured here at the inner docks at Hull pending her evening departure to Zeebrugge following her extensive refit in 2002. She has been renamed ***Pride of York.*** *(Miles Cowsill)*

Above: The ***Louise Russ*** was originally acquired for a new ferry service between Southampton, Oporto and Tangiers. Following the operation closing in Autumn 2001, she was returned to her German owners and was further chartered to Cobelfret Ferries and placed on their Rotterdam-Immingham service. The vessel operates still in her original livery and is seen here inward bound in the New Waterway from Immingham. *(Rob de Visser)*

Below: The elderly ***Stena Searider*** was transferred to the Harwich Hook of Holland service in 1997. Some three years later she inaugurated a new ferry service between the Hook of Holland and Killingholme near Immingham. *(John Bryant)*

Above: The ***Baltic Eider*** is pictured at Felixstowe pending her departure to Amsterdam for Finnlines. *(John Hendy)*

Below: Norfolkline's ***Maersk Exporter*** (pictured) and the ***Maersk Importer***, both built in Japan, currently maintain the Felixstowe-Scheveningen service. The vessel is seen here at Felixstowe. *(John Hendy)*

An impressive view of the ***Stena Hollandica*** in a floating dry dock in Holland undergoing her annual overhaul. *(Rob de Visser)*

Above: The ***Dana Anglia*** is pictured here inward bound from Esbjerg prior to receiving sponsons to her hull. DFDS transferred the ***Dana Anglia*** from the Harwich-Esbjerg service in September 2002 to their new Polish service and renamed the vessel ***Duke of Scandinavia***. Fierce competition from cheap air travel in recent years has made the traditional Esbjerg service less attractive to passengers. *(John Hendy)*

Below: The ***Explorer 12*** currently maintains the estuary ferry service between Harwich and Felixstowe. *(John Bryant)*

Right: Mann Lines operate a freight service between Harwich, Cuxhaven, Tallinn and Bremerhaven using the ***Estraden***. The Finnish built vessel is seen here arriving off Harwich. *(Roger Hurford)*

Below: Following the withdrawal of the ***Dana Anglia*** from the Harwich-Esbjerg service, the ro-pax vessel ***Dana Gloria*** took her place. The Danish company plan to introduce a larger vessel on the route during 2003. *(DFDS)*

Above: Following Stena Line withdrawing their interest from P&O Stena Line at Dover, P&O's operations between Felixstowe and Europort and Zeebrugge were acquired by the Swedish company. The former ***European Tideway*** is pictured here in her new Stena Line livery following the takeover as the ***Ideway***. She has since been renamed the ***Stena Transfer***. *(William Mayes)*

Above: The ***Gaelic Ferry*** is seen here in her splendid ASN livery leaving Felixstowe for Europort. The service established by ASN was taken over by Townsend Thoresen in 1971 and subsequently was operated by P&O. Following reorganisation of the P&O Group, the service was acquired by Stena Line in 2002. *(Ferry Publications Library)*

Below: This interesting aerial view shows the ***Doric Ferry*** at her berth loading for Europort with her converted sister the ***Nordic Ferry*** leaving for Zeebrugge. The Felixstowe Zeebrugge passenger service was inaugurated by Townsend Thoresen using the ***Viking II*** and subsequently the ***Viking Viscount*** and ***Viking Voyager.*** The passenger service closed in 1995 following continued losses on the link. *(FotoFlite)*

Top Right: This view shows the ***Viking Viscount*** and her sister the ***Viking Voyager*** passing each other during their first season on the Felixstowe-Zeebrugge route. Both vessels today are still in operation; the ***Viking Viscount*** currently operates between Crete and the mainland of Greece whilst her sister, the 'Voyager', is employed in the Canary Islands. *(FotoFlite)*

Right: The ***St. Edmund*** was built for the Harwich-Hook service by Sealink. The vessel remains in service today operating between Spain and Morocco. During her interesting career, including operations in the Falklands War, she was to be the largest vessel ever to operate between the UK and the Channel Islands. The vessel is pictured as the ***Rozel*** whilst operating for British Channel Island Ferries on page 54. *(FotoFlite)*

Below: The ***Koningin Beatrix*** was ordered by SMZ for their Hook of Holland-Harwich service. The vessel is seen here in Crown Line livery. Following the takeover of the route by Stena Line, she was eventually transferred from the route on the entry into service of the ***Stena Discovery***. She was to spend four years on the Fishguard-Rosslare service until 2002 when she was transferred to Stena Line's Polish route. *(Ferry Publications Library)*

DFDS SEAWAY

The ***Dana Gloria*** is pictured here shortly after her acquisition by DFDS. Today she operates for Fjord Line as the ***Jupiter*** - see page 113. *(FotoFlite)*

INDEX

The ***Isle of Arran*** inward bound from Islay. *(Miles Cowsill)*

The 25 knot ***SeaFrance Rodin*** departs from Calais during her first couple of weeks in service with the company. *(John Hendy)*

INDEX

The ***Pride of Calais*** is pictured here in the new P&O Ferries livery inward bound from her major refit in February 2003. *(FotoFlite)*

ACKNOWLEDGEMENTS

The authors are grateful to all those who have assisted with this publication. A special word of thanks should go to David and Dorothy Parsons for kindly offering to read the proofs. The following are thanked for use of their photographic material: Colin Smith, John Bryant, William Mayes, Roger Hurford, Matthew Punter, Rob de Visser, Barry Mitchell, Anthony Meads, Nicholas Meads, Willie Mackay, Gordon Hislip, Adrian Symons, John van der Linden and FotoFlite. Thanks also go to Andrew Lowe of Signature Design and to Pat Somner, who have assisted with this publication.